YOUR KNOWLEDGE HAS VALUE

Jurij Weinblat

Home server based personal archive management system

Analysis, design and specification of a Personal Information Archive Search

GRIN Publishing

Imprint:

Copyright © 2012 GRIN Verlag GmbH
Print and binding: Books on Demand GmbH, Norderstedt Germany
ISBN: 978-3-656-55355-7

This book at GRIN:

http://www.grin.com/en/e-book/265691/home-server-based-personal-archive-management-system

3. Functional description

The system is based on results of scientific research to benefit from their findings. It was observed that users use PIM to mainly retrieve emails, web pages, text and PowerPoint documents [6]. This means that the HS must support these formats as well as common email-applications and web browsers. Fuller et al. pointed out that the document's context information is often easier to remember than their actual content. Hence this information has to be both stored and related to the corresponding documents. The authors have also described how to organize context information in XML files. To do this the event concept has been introduced. An event can be for instance the opening or printing of the corresponding file. Each event is stored together with meta information like its start time, the current weather and the current user's position [2]. Apart from these properties it makes sense to integrate the user's calendar from Applications like Microsoft Outlook and Google Calendar.

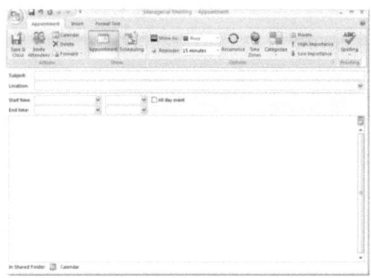
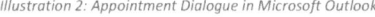

Illustration 2: Appointment Dialogue in Microsoft Outlook

Illustration 3: Example of document preview

Illustration 2 depicts that such appointments do not only embody the appointment's name and date but also its location and the involved people. If a certain Word document was created during a certain management meeting which took place in Glasgow and was attended by five people this information can probably be used as context information for this document for later retrieval. However, a disadvantage is that a normal email that arrives during this appointment is going to be classified wrongly. Furthermore it makes sense to store properties which users remember most likely. In this context it was discovered that users tend to remember attributes like location, file type and time of last usage [7].

To store this information the open source search system Lucene can be used because it has the necessary functionality according to [2] and [8]. Especially it supports Cross-format search which improves the applicability of a search engine [9]. Lucene has a relatively big community and was already used in real projects. However it is a standard software and most likely contains a lot of functionality which will never be used and reduces the performance of the system.

Furthermore using a standard software means that only the algorithms which are offered by this software can be used for retrieval. Nevertheless it is still necessary to select an algorithm to summarize the retrieved documents and present them to the user to support him to assess the relevance of the individual documents. Summaries, which take the query into account, were identified as being more constructive than query independent summaries [10] and small preview pictures of the retrieved documents are helpful, too. As not only the first page should be previewed the PIM tool should enable the user to click through the previews without opening the document. Illustration 3 is an example of such a preview.

4. Implementation plan

It is crucial to explain how the HS both collects new documents from the user's devices, register new events and retrieves all kinds of documents. To enable PCs and laptops to send documents to the HS and register events, a special background software (BS) should be used, which has to be installed on every device. This software should support plugins like it is done in [11]. Every plugin "tells" the software how to cope with a certain file format or application. This has the advantage that the programmer of every tool knows best how to handle their tools or files and that the BS becomes modular and easier to implement. On the other hand, the success of the HS will depend on the fact how many developers will create these plugins for their tools. This is why it makes sense to include the developer of the most relevant tools in the development of the HS. In order to integrate smartphones and tablet PCs special Apps should be written, which also run in the background and can be enchased by plugins. The HS should provide a well-described interface to communicate with the BS and apps. This interface should accept incoming documents and events but deny access to stored documents in the HDM. The only way to access these documents and to formulate queries is the usage of the web interface within the home network or over the Internet over an URL using a Dynamic DNS service [12].

This web interface should also allow the user to download plugins for the HS itself to enable it to deal with more file formats. Another field of application of the HS' plugins is the access to web services like Facebook and Dropbox to download their content as well. The architecture is depicted in Illustration 4. To connect for instance the Email client Thunderbird to the HS two plugins are re-

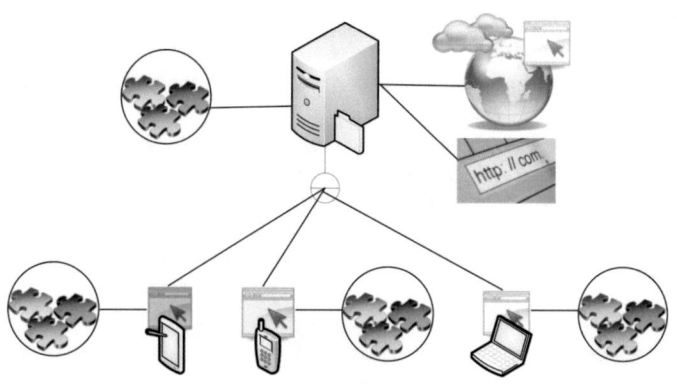

Illustration 4: Plugin architecture

quired: One for the HS and one for the BS on the computer.

The disadvantage of this architecture is to identify the current user of a tablet PC, which is used by several household members, in order to relate for example a viewed website only to this user. Moreover it would not be allowed to install the BS on the user's PC at his workplace as corporate documents would be copied to the HS and could not be deleted by the company any longer [13].

5. Evaluation plan

According to the lecture notes, IR systems can be evaluated quantitatively and qualitatively. Within the **quantitative** evaluation the indices "Recall" and "Precision" play a significant role but it is often unrealistic to improve both indices at the same time because of their trade-off relationship [14]. The improvement of the Recall should be prioritized in for the HS to make sure that if the user searches a certain document it will be most likely found. Nevertheless Precision is relevant, too, as a high precision saves the user's time to find the relevant document(s) within the result list.

The fact that the HS is a PIM system has important implications for the **qualitative** evaluation: The user must search within his own documents to simulate a realistic scenario and his privacy must be protected. Both of these implications are considered by Jones and Chen who propose to install the PIM system on the user's computer and let him perform retrieval tasks and evaluate them. In order to find out if the integration of a calendar improves the performance of the search it has to be made sure, that some of the users use a supported calendar application actively [11]. The effectiveness of the preview feature can be determined by the use of surveys.

Another evaluation approach is to measure if and how many files, which were retrieved, were opened by the user [6]. By logging the origin of opened files it can be determined if the user actively tries to retrieve documents from his mobile devices and web services and not only his local computer. This indicates to a certain extent if there is a need for a HS.

Nevertheless these approaches are still not completely realistic as such HS would normally be used for years and not only for months. Thus the HDM will be bigger and its items will be worse remembered [2].

6. Conclusion

This paper illustrates the concept of a HS which combines advantages of a local storage and a cloud based storage and avoids their crucial disadvantages. The relevant multimedia documents from devices like PCs, smartphones, tablets and also from web services are stored at a single place and can be therefore retrieved centrally. Moreover this concept considers several best practices like the use of metadata as an additional source of information to retrieve relevant documents. The unique features of the HS are the calendar integration and the easy preview of the retrieved documents. The system can be enhanced with plugins to enable developers to make their own tools compatible with the HS.

However the system has several disadvantages, too, which should be addressed in future research: Used on devices where it is not obvious which household member is currently using them (like tablets or laptops without distinct accounts for every user) the HS will not be able to assign used documents to a specific user. Moreover it will most likely not be permitted to install the BS on a company's computer because it will store the company's confidential documents (which were used by the employee) in a place where they are not accessible by the company any more. As people usually use a significant number of private documents at their company's computer as well, not being able to retrieve them would be a significant problem for a system, which is supposed to store all the user's memories.

7. List of references

[1] L. Kelly, Y. Chen, M. Fuller and G. J. Jones, "A Study of Remembered Context for Information Access," in *Information Interaction in Context*, London, UK, 2008.

[2] M. Fuller, L. Kelly and G. J. Jones, "Applying Contextual Memory Cues for Retrieval from," in *Proceedings of Personal Information Management*, Dublin, Ireland, 2008.

[3] ZDNet, "ZDNet," 2012. [Online]. Available: http://www.zdnet.com/topic-laptops/. [Accessed 29 11 2012].

[4] Electronista, "Electronista," Electronista, 17 11 2009. [Online]. Available: http://www.electronista.com/articles/09/11/17/reliability.study.has.apple.4th.place/. [Accessed 29 11 2012].

[5] B. Sosinsky, Cloud Computing Bible, Indianapolis, Indiana: Wiley Publishing, Inc, 2011.

[6] S. Dumais, E. Cutrell, J. Cadiz, G. Jancke, R. Sarin and D. C. Robbins, "Stuff I've Seen: A System for Personal Information Retrieval and Re-Use," in *Proceedings of the 26th annual international ACM SIGIR conference on Research and development in informaion retrieval*, New York, USA, 2003.

[7] T. Blanc-Brude and D. L. Scapin, "What do People Recall about their Documents? Implications for Desktop Search Tools," in *Proceedings of the 12th international conference on Intelligent user interfaces* , New York, USA, 2007.

[8] The Apache Software Foundation, "Apache Lucene Core," The Apache Software Foundation, 2012-2012. [Online]. Available: http://lucene.apache.org/core/index.html. [Accessed 4 12 2012].

[9] O. Bergman, R. Beyth-Marom, R. Nachmias, N. Gradovitch and S. Whittaker, "Improved Search Engines and Navigation Preference in Personal Information Management," *ACM Transactions on Information Systems,* pp. 20-43, 9 2008.

[10] G. J. Jones, *Lecture notes for Multimedia Information Retrieval (CA437) - Summarization,* Dublin, Irland: Dublin City Iniversity, 2012.

[11] G. J. F. Jones and Y. Chen, "A Strategy for Evaluating Search of "Real" Personal Information Archives," in *Proceedings of the fifth ACM international conference on Web search and data mining*, New York, USA, 2012.

[12] ITBusinessEdge, "dynamic DNS," ITBusinessEdge, 2012. [Online]. Available: http://www.webopedia.com/TERM/D/dynamic_DNS.html. [Accessed 05 12 2012].

[13] G. Bell, J. Gemmell and R. Lueder, "Challenges in Using Lifetime Personal Information Stores," in *Proceedings of the 27th annual international ACM SIGIR conference on Research and development in information retrieval*, New York, USA, 2004.

[14] G. J. F. Jones, *Lecture notes for Multimedia Information Retrieval (CA437) - Text Retrieval,* Dublin, Ireland: Dublin City University, 2012.